WELCOME TO YOUR UNIVERSAL CONSCIOUSNESS JOURNAL

The universal consciousness chakra, sometimes known as the eighth chakra or soul star. It is located above the head and is the centre of enlightenment, ascension, letting go divine light and the ancient knowledge of the soul.

Each page has space for you to reflect on an idea, theme, or issue based on the Chakra Card questions in the accompanying Chakra Card decks.

This is the final chakra in the series and once this chakra is cleared, the possibilities are infinite.

There are three tips for using this journal:
1. Be honest with yourself. This book will not be read by others unless you allow it.
2. Before writing, meditate on the sacral chakra and write from that space, try and get out of your head, get into your body.
3. Let emotions flow, and allow whatever comes to come. Be a witness to it. However, should you require extra support, please reach out to your favoured mental health professional.

Happy writing!

www.alyssacurtayne.com

CHAKRA NINE
UNIVERSAL CONSCIOUSNESS CHAKRA

How do you know when you are on the right path?

What surprised you today?

How do you know when you are communicating with your higher self?

Who, or what, is I?

Meditation: make your mind as vast as the sky, as expansive as the universe and sit in this energy.

Will you return to Earth after this incarnation?

Consider the word: 'contentment'.
What does it feel like to you?

What does ascension mean to you?

How can you be a conscious, global participant in the Earth family?

What do you understand to be "Christ Consciousness"?

Reflect on your meditative practices.

Who or what has been your greatest teacher?

How can you serve humanity and life on Earth?

Affirm: I am made of love and light. Does any resistance come up for you?

In what areas of your life do you feel that you need permission to shine?

___
___
___
___
___
___
___
___
___
___
___
___
___
___
___
___
___
___
___
___

How do you become hesitant in uplifting others?

How do you know when you are operating from your soul?

What emotionally touched or moved you today?

We are told we live in a world of dualities (sun/moon, masculine/feminine). Discuss.

My purpose is to...

What do you know about past lives? Are you ready to get them all go now?

How can you love yourself more?

How are you being the inspiration you wish you had?

What are you seeing about yourself in the reflections of others in your life?

The secret to life is...

What inspired you today?

What are you denying?

What do you still need to experience? How will you know when you are finished?

How do you nurture your physical body; the temple that houses your soul?

_____
_____
_____
_____
_____
_____
_____
_____
_____
_____
_____
_____
_____
_____
_____
_____
_____
_____

What have all relationships with others taught you?

What is faith?

What more do you need to let go of?

Affirm: I clearly see the divine plan for myself and this planet.

When I die, I will go satisfied knowing that I...

The Akashic records are said to hold all of your ancient knowledge, what do you know?

What would you like to manifest?

What karmic patterns are you still playing out?

How do you show humility?

When you see events happening in the world, how do you respond?

My human experience is, and has been...

What challenged you today?

What do you still have to learn?

What does it mean to be "spiritual"?

What have been your greatest achievements?

Affirmation: "I am a divine creator."

Love is...

How do you use your energetic field? Do you have a conscious awareness of energy?

Visualise yourself as every living and non-living being on Earth.

Time and space is complex and yet simple, how do you view it in the context of the human experience?

How do you practice non-attachment in your life?

Can you move beyond the material world? Do you want to?

Have you let go of the victim-mindset?

How can you expand your heart's light into the world?

Reflection

Date: _____

Return to the start and re-read your previous entries

_____
_____
_____

Do you notice any recurring themes or ideas?

_____
_____
_____

What were you surprised by?

_____
_____
_____

I exist

The final page

This practice has taught me

_____
_____
_____
_____

I am, just because I exist.

I exist

All rights reserved. No part of this book may be used or reproduced by any means, graphic, electronic, or mechanical, including photocopying, recording, taping or by any information storage retrieval system without the written permission of the copyright owner.
First edition published 2016 by Alyssa Curtayne, this edition published in Australia by Rising Spirit; Where Great Ideas Grow and Alyssa Curtayne, © 2023.

I exist

www.ingramcontent.com/pod-product-compliance
Lightning Source LLC
Chambersburg PA
CBHW040743020526
44107CB00084B/2848